Marcel Vrignaud

My Ikebana

Marcel Vrignaud

My Ikebana

stichting kunstboek

Rudbeckia - Rosa - Chamaerops

OHARA SCHOOL OF IKEBANA

Preface

It certainly is gratifying for all of us who enjoy ikebana that today it is practiced throughout the nations. It is not only because of its esthetic and philosophical value but also of being a good therapy for us who lead our lives in such a busy world. It has adapted the indigenous culture, customs and floral materials of various countries. I am proud of saying that ikebana has contributed to strengthen international understanding and goodwill through love for flowers.

It is my pleasure to write the preface to this book entitled “My Ikebana,” featuring the excellent compositions Mr. Marcel Vrignaud has created in the past five years. Since it also presents the names of floral materials and explanations for containers used in each composition, ikebana lovers may find an idea of interesting material-container combinations to their own compositions.

Mr. Marcel Vrignaud started his ikebana career in Nagoya, Japan under late Professor Kodo Kanamori of the Council of Ohara Professors in 1963. Intrigued by the lure of Ohara ikebana, he stayed in Japan to continue his advanced studies under several prominent professors. He of course did his advanced studies under late third Headmaster Houn Ohara in Kobe.

After returning to France, he founded the France Chapter in 1967 and has since led the Chapter as its President. His distinguished nearly 50-year devotion to the Ohara School is deeply admired and appreciated. In 2009, he was honored by the Ohara School to receive the Award of Honor (Meiyo-Ichijikin), an exceptional honor granted to outstanding Ohara Masters, and has become a lifetime Honorary Member of the Ohara School.

I would like to take this opportunity to convey my congratulations on the publication of this book. I am certain that it will play the important role of bridge among those interested in ikebana especially in Europe to make them closely linked to Ohara ikebana.

Wakako Ohara

Wakako Ohara
Chief Executive

Rosa - Viburnum opulus - Sophora japonica

Anthurium - Dracaena massangeana - Wild lonicera creeper

Heliconia - Hosta - Heracleum sphondylium

Anthurium - Pandanus

Hosta - Lilium - Celosia cristata

Helianthus - Alpinia purpurata - Spartium junceum

 Fresh squash - Hippeastrum

Chrysanthemum - Various fresh squash - Choiysia ternata - Hydrangea - Gladiolus - Wisteria creeper - Bamboo

Scindapsus aureus (pothos) - Dried squash - Heliconia caribaea

Anthurium - Aspidistra

Anthurium - Dried squash - Cotoneaster horizontalis - Conifer

Hosta - Typha latifolia variegata - Lilium

Fraxinus - Helianthus - Gunnera manicata

Dried squash - Monstera - Anthurium - Bleached creeper

Heliconia caribaea - Bleached creeper - Moss of the woods

 Dried squash - Heliconia caribaea - Pandanus sanderi - Mitsumata - Protea nutans

Hosta - Heliconia caribaea - Euphorbia

 Lilium - Hosta - Strelitzia leaves - Ulmus campestris

Anthurium - Pandanus - Petrea volubilis

 Anthurium - Dry Sambucus - Calla - Musa

Anthurium - Alpinia leaves - Ulmus

 Hemerocallis - Polygonatum - Achillea - Acer

 Epilobium - Epicea - Alstroemeria - Vaccinium - Grass

Cydonia japonica - Rosa - Acer palmatum

Orchids - Chrysalidocarpus - Cercis siliquastrum - Arum italicum

Orchids - Acer - Prunus serrulata (sakura)

Rosa - Lilium - Chrysanthemum - Hosta - Aster

Fresh squash - Lilium - Euonymus europaeus - Dried mushrooms - Castanea

Dahlia - Hydrangea - Ricinus

 Viola - Botanical Tulipa leaves - Spirea

Chrysanthemum - Hydrangea quercifolia

 Cydonia japonica - Camellia - Conifer

Calla - Rhododendron - Iris leaves

 Anthurium - Sorbus aucuparia - Angelica archangelica

Azalea - Wisteria - Lisianthus

 Chrysanthemum - Prunus spinosa - Quercus rubra

Hemerocallis - Ligularia - Stewartia pseudocamellia

 Small Chrysanthemum - Celosia - Lilium - Heracleum leaves - Limonium

Calla - Rosa canina - Lonicera periclymenum - Hosta

 Mahonia actifolium - Camellia - Chrysanthemum - Cydonia japonica - Arum italicum

Cytisus laburnum - Paeonia lactiflora

Nelumbo nucifera - Calla - Iris

Nelumbo nucifera - Miscanthus

 Petunia - Heuchera - Pelargonium - Chelidonium majus

Crocosmia - Hemerocallis - Pelargonium

Achillea - Zea mays leaves - Dipsacus fullonum

Typha latifolia - Hydrangea - Petasites

 Polygonatum - Rosa canina - Celosia cristata - Chrysanthemum - Limonium - Sambucus racemosa

Quercus rubra - Chrysanthemum - Ulmus

 Celosia argentea - Hosta - Rosa - Amaranthus caudatus - Salvia

Fuschia - Fern - Rudbeckia

 Wisteria - Iris germanica - Azalea - Ligularia

Hosta - *Hibiscus moscheutos*

Iris - Hosta - Azalea - Malus

Hosta - Paeonia - Hemerocallis - Hydrangea - Euonymus

Cercis siliquastrum - Fern - Syringa

 Lilium - Hydrangea - Hosta - Delphinium - Paeonia

Fuschia - Dahlia - Bergenia

Bignonia - Acer - Helianthus - Perovskia

Ricinus - Dahlia - Ligularia - Phytolacca

Polygonatum - Typha - Gunnera - Arum italicum

Helianthus - Dracaena massangeana - Cornus sanguinea

Nelumbo nucifera

 Chrysanthemum - Azalea - Paeonia - Viburnum plicatum

Lilium - Cornus kousa - Small Chrysanthemum

 Epicea - Erica - Mountain flowers

Polygonatum - Achillea - Arctium

 Azalea - Pinus - Pontederia - Calla - Salvia

Hibiscus moscheutos - Hydrangea - Miscanthus

 Anthurium - Musa - Gloriosa superba - Anacardium occidentale

Anthurium - Pandanus - Orchids

Canna - Datura - Salvia

Pelargonium - Prunus pissardii

 Kerria japonica - Magnolia stellata - Camellia - Musa - Orchids

Iris - Lilium - Fagus sylvatica - Polygonatum - Celosia cristata - Statice sinuata - Chrysanthemum

Gerbera - Angelica archangelica - Dried Fagus branches

Orchids - Aralia - Codiaeum variegatum

Malus - Nelumbo nucifera - Lilium

Fritillaria imperialis - Forsythia fortunei - Aesculus hippocastanum

 Orchids - Wisteria - Prunus serrulata - Spirea - Acer - Cornus

Prunus serrulata - Lilium - Aesculus hippocastanum

 Conifer - Hemerocallus - Aesculus indica - Narcissus - Amelanchier ovalis

Bignonia - Sorbus aucuparia

 Dahlia - Alcea rosea

Rosa canina - Verbascum phlomoides - Pelargonium leaves

 Gladiolus - Pandanus - Solidago - Larix europea

Sophora - Hosta - Lilium

 Acer - Rosa - Prunus pissardii

Petasites leaves - Alpinia purpurata - Angelica

 Iris germanica - Rosa - Rhodendron - Acer - Houttuynia cordata

Nelumbo nucifera - Nandina domestica - Lilium

 Cydonia japonica - Arum italicum - Oncidium

Calla - Sedum - Cydonia oblonga

 Wisteria floribunda - Iris - Fern

Oncidium - Mahonia aquifolium - Tillandsia - Paeonia

 Hemerocallis - Hydrangea - Salix contorta

Iris leaves - Viola - Azalea

Paeonia - Magnolia stellata - Mahonia japonica

Celosia - Aralia leaves - Dry Eucalyptus - Datura

Celosia - Hydrangea - Polygonatum - Solidago

Calla - Celosia cristata - Castanea - Fresh squash - Wild lonicera creeper

Canna - Dahlia - Fuchsia

 Lilium - Cydonia japonica - Amelanchier ovalis

Heliconia caribaea - Acanthus - Rudbeckia - Aralia

 Polygonatum - Castanea - Pyracantha - Euonymus

 Strelitzia - Azalea - Heuchera - Triticum

Hosta - Iris germanica - Celosia cristata

Nymphea - Allamanda cathartica - Pachystachys lutea - Congea tomentosa

Rhapis excelsa - Punica granatum - Hibiscus

 Strelitzia - Iris - Hemerocallis

 Myosotis - Hemerocallis - Viola

Hosta - Chrysanthemum - Hydrangea - Papaver

Celosia - Aralia leaves - Dry Eucalyptus - Ageratum

Hydrangea - Castanea - Angelica leaves

 Cotoneaster horizontalis - Squash - Ampelopsis leaves - Helianthus

Hosta - Gladiolus - Celosia

 Iris germanica - Paeonia - Weigelia - Cercis siliquastrum

Acer - Petasites - Epilobium

Nelumbo nucifera leaf - Helianthus - Ricinus - Rosa

Lilium - Hosta - Dried Helianthus - Solanum lycopersicum

Lilium - Hydrangea - Euonymus europaeus

 Pandanus leaf - Helianthus - Delphinium - Codiaeum

Acer - Azalea - Camellia

 Iris germanica - Hosta - Cytisus

Chrysanthemum - Juglans regia - Euonymus

 Hemerocallis - Magnolia stellata - Cydonia japonica - Driftwood - Tillandsia - Musa

Lilium - Fern - Wisteria floribunda

 Centaurea - Pelargonium leaves - Azalea

Lisianthus - Hosta - Weigelia - Paeonia

 Lilium - Ricinus - Driftwood

Forsythia - Camellia - Aesculus hippocastanum

 Polygonatum - Celosia cristata - Pinus - Fagus - Lisianthus - Statice

Musa - Magnolia stellata - Chrysanthemum - Cydonia japonica

Lilium - Cydonia japonica - Polypodium punctatum

Dracaena massangeana - Delphinium - Viburnum opulus

 Viburnum opulus - Chrysanthemum - Tillandsia - Malus - Castanea

Spirea - Nelumbo nucifera - Nymphea - Ligularia leaves

 Cydonia japonica - Grataegus - Conifer - Arum italicum

Solidago - Acer - Hydrangea

 Hemerocallis - Bignonia - Euonymus - Gentiana

Azalea - Calla - Chrysalidocarpus

 Dracaena massangeana – Calla – Pandanus – Delphinium – Lonicera creeper

Chrysanthemum - Cercis siliquastrum - Hydrangea quercifolia

 Fuschia - Rosa - Lisianthus

Gladiolus - Phytolacca americana - Foeniculum

Nelumbo nucifera

Acer palmatum - Nymphea - Azalea - Sorbus aucuparia

 Ixora - Combretum rotundifolium - Phoenix canariensis

Phoenix canariensis - Philodendron - Nymphea

 Houttuynia cordata - Pelargonium - Nymphea - Scirpus

Lilium - Dry Conifer - Rosa canina - Wild Pelargonium

 Iris - Rosa - Azalea - Philodendron - Hydrangea quercifolia

Caladium - Orchids - Philodendron - Acacia

 Hosta - Chrysanthemum - Celosia cristata - Typha latifolia variegata

Hydrangea - Lilium

Marcel Vrignaud is the founder and permanent professor of the Ikebana Floral Art Center, an association he set up in 1966 after spending three and a half years in Nagoya in Japan, devoted to the specific art of Ikebana (floral arrangements based on Japanese techniques and traditions).

This genuine pioneer trained teachers all over Europe. His students frequently come from afar to follow his courses. His school offers a comprehensive teaching programme in this art through workshops, thematic visits to Paris, the provinces and abroad, professional training sessions, exhibitions and public demonstrations.

After climbing all the rungs in the ladder of this age-old art in Japan, he returned to France at a time when Ikebana was still unknown. Today, the association has an average of 450 permanent members throughout France, its overseas departments and other countries in Europe, not to mention the students of the numerous teachers he trained, who in turn coordinate their own groups all over the country.

He obtained the highest awards and distinctions from the Japanese Grand Masters of this discipline:

- Diploma of the horticultural schools of Nantes and Versailles,
- Founding President of the Ohara-France Chapter in 1967 on the recommendation of the *Iemoto* Hôun Ohara,
- Ikebana Grand Master since about thirty years,
- Kôrô Shô, a Japanese diploma of merit, which he shares with only one other Westerner,
- International demonstrator,
- Columnist for the magazine "Esprit Bonsaï", and author of books and articles,
- Founding member of the Floral Art Section of the Société Nationale d'Horticulture de France and member of the European Ohara Teachers Association,
- Holder of the French National Order of Merit, awarded for his achievements in disseminating the art of Ikebana in France,
- Honorary member for life of the Ohara School in Japan,
- Meiyo Ichijikin (Award of Honour), an honorary distinction awarded by Japan in 2009 in recognition of services rendered to the teaching and promotion of Ikebana in Europe.

His lengthy technical and educational experience is a guarantee of the high standard of his teaching. Marcel Vrignaud shows great respect and attention to his students; he is more indulgent with beginners but stricter and more demanding with advanced students, teachers and masters.

He is frequently requested to conduct workshops and demonstrations and to prepare floral exhibitions in France and its overseas departments, as well as other parts of Europe and Japan. He has organized Ikebana study trips to Japan, China, South Africa, Madagascar, Philippines, Greece, Martinique, Guyana, Guadeloupe and other countries.

The work in 'My Ikebana' illustrates a series of bouquets created during the last ten years, photographed during summer seminars and workshops overseas, in studios, the Parc Floral de la Court d'Aron in the Vendée and the Jardins des Renaudies in Mayenne.

Readers may discover many original combinations of plants, gathered during different seasons, and displayed in the most unusual containers, reflecting all the categories of bouquets of the Ohara School: moribana, heika, landscapes, rimpa, bunjin, morimono, free style, Ikebana sculpture, micro Ikebana, transparencies, etc.

- Centre d'Art Floral Ikebana - Ohara-France Chapter
  26 rue Armaillé, 75017 Paris
  centre-cafi@orange.fr
  www.ikebana-ohara.fr

Creations
Marcel Vrignaud
www.ikebana-ohara.fr

Photography
Marcel Vrignaud

Photo editing
Patrice Lahaye (studio Pat. Houdan)

Final editing
Katrien Van Moerbeke

Lay-out
www.groupvandamme.eu

Print
www.pureprint.be

Published by
Stichting Kunstboek bvba
Legeweg 165
B-8020 Oostkamp
T. +32 50 46 19 10
F. +32 50 46 19 18
info@stichtingkunstboek.com
www.stichtingkunstboek.com

ISBN 978-90-5856-401-6
D/2011/6407/28
NUR 421